World War 2 History's

10 Most Incredible

Women

World War II True Accounts Of Remarkable Women
Heroes

By

Stephanie T McRae

©2016

Contents

Introduction

The intent of this book, in part, is simply to remember the forgotten heroes of World War II, recognizing that many of the remarkable accomplishments of the era may be attributed to the skill and expertise of a band of sisters. In the following pages, a photographer, an historian, a driver, several professional spies, and multiple nurses are profiled as seemingly fearless women. However, like the male soldiers they served beside, they were not fearless. Rather, they overcame their fear and faced adversity to serve a greater cause: freedom.

While the popular image of "Rosie the Riveter" rightfully endures, women's contributions to the war effort cover an expanse of roles. Certainly, they filled "traditional" female roles such as cook, secretary, seamstress, nurse, and morale booster (not a task to be taken lightly). They also served as front-line documentarians, doctors, pilots, fighters, intelligence officers, and indeed, leaders.

It is interesting to note that several of the women profiled here came from privileged backgrounds, or otherwise found themselves in a position of privilege as the war broke out. The worldwide conflict equalized their circumstances however, as none of them survived the war easily, and many did not survive. These heroines' contributions to the war effort put each of them in mortal danger. They were injured, tortured or killed. Those that survived the trauma of war in some cases relived it for the rest of their lives.

Margaret Bourke-White, Virginia Hall, Rose Valland, Elsie Ott, Aleda Lutz, Susan Travers, Eileen Nearne, Jacqueline Nearne, Claire Phillips, and Nancy Wake: their sacrifices are more than worthy of recognition. Their heroism is something that should not be forgotten.

I *Margaret Bourke-White*
(1904-1971)

Were it not for photographer Margaret Bourke-White, the heroism of many of the women profiled in this book may not have been noticed. Certainly, it is largely due to her fearless documenting of the immediate horrors of conflict, the lost lives and destruction, that those remaining on the home-front, and in administrators' offices, were able to intellectualize the conflict around the world. It was not a tidy Hollywood movie, with singing troops marching happily to their deaths. It was lost limbs, and overwhelming destruction; indeed, it was death incarnate. Yet the chaos of war was an inescapable draw for Margaret Bourke-White, a woman born to chase through her photographer's lenses, that solitary moment in time that can be worth a thousand words - or in Bourke-White's case, could represent a thousand lives.

Bourke-White was born "Margaret White" in Brooklyn, NY in 1904, and reared by Jewish and Irish-Catholic parents in New Jersey. (As an adult she adopted and hyphenated her mother's surname to that of her father.) Bourke-White's first camera was gifted to her by her mother. Almost immediately, she developed an affinity for photographing inanimate objects, architecture, and mechanical systems.

Indecisive toward her studies, Bourke-White attended seven universities before graduating with an A.B. from Cornell. To support herself throughout her college years, Bourke-White sold photographs that focused primarily on campus architecture and scenery, wherever she happened to study.

Her widowed mother had relocated to Cleveland, Ohio, and following graduation, and a brief marriage and subsequent divorce from Everett Chapman, Bourke-White joined her there.

As a freelance photographer, Bourke-White continued to focus on architectural subjects as well as industrial subjects, and to a lesser extent, advertising. A series of photographs of Ohio steel mills brought her some renown, and in 1929, she was hired as the first photographer for a new magazine, *Fortune.*

This began a series of notable "firsts" for Bourke-White, eventually leading to distinctions as the first female photojournalist, first photo essayist, first unrestricted photographer allowed in the Soviet Union, first female war correspondent, and later, to recognition as a pioneer of industrial photography. Bourke-White's affiliation with *Fortune* also marked the beginning of a transitional period for her from inanimate subjects to those of flesh and blood.

Her most notable works included a series on Depression-era Dust Bowl farmers, and *You Have Seen Their Faces*, a book published jointly with second husband Erskine Caldwell, that depicted struggling southern sharecroppers. In 1936, she became a staff photographer at *Life* magazine, a position which garnered her fame as the artist whose work graced the cover of the first magazine, and fame as a seemingly fearless *documentarienne*.

Bourke-White had travelled independently, prior to the outbreak of war, to Europe to document burgeoning Nazism in Germany, Austria, and Czechoslovakia. Whether she was aware of the consequences or not, being of Jewish heritage, the trip was a dangerous move for the photographer, but her work nevertheless told an invaluable story to those outside the Nazi world. In 1941, she travelled to the Soviet Union to document the Soviet people's preparation for the pending German invasion, and found herself in a bombarded Moscow as the Germans arrived. There is some question as to whether Bourke-White photographed the bombardment from the relative safety of the U.S. Embassy, or whether she set her equipment in the window of her hotel to photograph automatically and then retreated to the hotel's basement. Regardless, Bourke-White's photography provided to the West one of the earliest non-filtered pictures of the Soviet predicament.

Life magazine negotiated an agreement with the Pentagon to allow Bourke-White to travel to war-torn Europe, initially to photograph the U.S. Air Force. Restricted to briefings, practice missions, and other events suitable for a lady that did not involve combat, Bourke-White chafed at the double-standard set for her and her male colleagues. She pressed for inclusion in battle assignments, and eventually General Jimmy Doolittle gave Bourke-White permission to cover the war in North Africa. Nevertheless, Bourke-White was required to travel by sea rather than facing the danger of air travel, and was sent via the British troopship *SS Strathallen* to cross the Mediterranean. Burke-White's transport was torpedoed mid-trip, and she found herself, and a lone surviving camera she'd managed to rescue, adrift with the soldiers clinging to lifeboats.

Perhaps it is this scrape with danger, and Bourke-White remaining unfazed by it, that convinced General Doolittle to acquiesce to her request to join combat runs. The General granted her the vantage point of a B-17 mission behind enemy lines. Bourke-White photographed the bombing alongside the bombardier in the close confines of the bomb bay. Her mission was successful: Margaret got the shots, and the mission destroyed over 100 German planes on the ground. Though her B-17 was hit by enemy fire, she and the crew made it back to base to discover that two planes on the mission had been destroyed.

Margaret Bourke-White later became an official photographer for the U.S. Army. Over the course of her service in the war, she flew with Allied bombing raids in Germany, over El Auina in Tunisia, North Africa, and above the Cassino Valley in Italy. At the close of the war, she was attached to General George S. Patton's Third Army as it travelled through crumbling Germany. Bourke-White was immediately on the heels of Patton and his Army as it opened the gates of Buchenwald concentration camp for the world to see. Margaret's photographs taken at Buchenwald introduced much of the world to a horror it had not previously contemplated. Her images of local townspeople forced by Patton to witness the carnage are haunting. A photograph taken of prisoners at Buchenwald's gates (that was not published until the 1960s) has become iconic of the wartime experience of millions of Jews. Her book *Purple Heart Valley* depicted the fighting in Italy. In *Dear Fatherland, Rest Quietly*, which Bourke-White is said to have undertaken as catharsis, chronicled her experience with the brutality of war.

Margaret Bourke-White enjoyed a long career after World War II, documenting conflict that dissolved many states and created new ones, from the Independence of India, to the Korean War. Her colleagues at *Life* gave her the nickname "Maggie the Indestructible". Sadly, she developed Parkinson's disease and it robbed her of the ability to engage in photography in the last years of her life. Margaret Bourke-White has been named one of the most important photographers of the Twentieth Century. She died in 1971 at the age of sixty-seven leaving an incredible body of work, having made an indelible impression on the art of photography and forever changing the public perception of war.

II *Virginia Hall*
(1906-1882)

Virginia Hall was a British intelligence agent, guerilla trainer, and American spy perhaps best known in the popular culture as the spy who was an amputee. A complex and well-educated woman, her actions were much more dangerous, and vital to the Allies, than the simplification of her as the "limping spy" allows.

Virginia Hall was born to privilege in 1906 in Baltimore, MD. Her parents travelled widely, exposing her to differing cultures early in life, and she developed a penchant for languages at an early age that would later serve her well. It is fitting that Hall also developed a longing to enter the U.S. Foreign Service, certainly in order to exercise and further develop her cultural skills, but also to quench a natural thirst for adventure. She studied at Harvard (Radcliffe), Columbia (Barnard), and multiple European institutions, developing fluency in French, German, and snippets of other languages. Despite her clear intelligence, Hall failed to pass the Foreign Service entrance exam twice, before finally landing a position in 1931 as a Consular Services clerk in the U.S. Embassy in Warsaw. Hall's intent was to prove her skills, and she hoped to advance to a more adventure-filled position quickly. However, the path she took to glory undoubtedly proved to be more circuitous than she envisioned.

While on a hunting trip to Turkey with friends, Hall's rifle misfired as she climbed a fence. The bullet tore through her foot and injured the surrounding tissues of the ankle and lower leg.

Gangrene subsequently forced doctors to amputate Hall's foot and the lowest part of her leg. Virginia resigned from the Foreign Service, returned to Baltimore, and spent almost a year there learning how to walk again on a custom wooden prosthesis she named "Cuthbert". Virginia and "Cuthbert" requested reinstatement to the Foreign Service and she once again headed to Europe for what proved to be a string of ungratifying clerical positions in Western Europe. When Germany invaded France in 1940, Hall once again left the Foreign Service to volunteer as an ambulance driver.

Hall later became SOE's first female operative to France. She worked in France over fifteen months helping prisoners escape from German and Vichy prisons, and training fighters in guerilla tactics. She spent much of her time, under a variety of aliases, disguised as an elderly milk maid, her limp and perceived age cloaking a master spy continuously eavesdropping on unsuspecting Germans. Hall worked with the French Underground until the Nazis seized all of France in 1942. She escaped to Spain on foot (one natural, one prosthetic), and after some difficulty transitioned to an unexciting undercover job in Madrid before being granted a transfer to London. In 1943, Hall was made an honorary MBE.

Hall departed SOE in 1944 to join the Office of Strategic Services (OSS). OSS sent her back to France on a British torpedo boat. Trained as a radio operator, Hall put her skills to work in central France coordinating parachute drops to resistance groups and recording German troop movements. She trained three battalions of French resistance fighters for sabotage missions, and though her identity was unknown, the Nazis launched an all-out effort to capture "Germaine", as Hall was known to the enemy, with Klause Barbie (later to be known as the Butcher of Lyon) leading the nationwide hunt. After the Allies invaded Normandy, Hall and her compatriots shifted from guerilla tactics to combat, even accepting the surrender of the German Southern Command at Le Chambon.

In 1945, Virginia Hall was awarded the Distinguished Service Cross. She was the only civilian woman in the war to receive this high honor. She continued her career in intelligence gathering and in 1956 became the first woman to become a member of the CIA's career staff and created modern intelligence gathering. Some have credited Hall as a pioneer of modern intelligence gathering, both for her prolific information gathering abilities, and for her unequaled ability to utilize disguise, creating the standard for hiding in clear sight.

III *Rose Valland*
(1898-1980)

While the Allies "Monuments Men" receive the bulk of the credit for returning and repatriating looted art, France's Rose Valland deserves a higher place in the public consciousness as she very well may have saved French culture from the Nazis. An art historian, member of the French Resistance, Captain in the French military, and long-time protector of cultural treasures, Valland photographed, catalogued, and subsequently identified thousands of stolen works; she risked her life for the art she loved.

Valland was educated in art and history, culminating in a degree from the Sorbonne. In 1932, unable to find an appropriate paying position, Valland became a volunteer assistant curator with the Jan de Paume Museum in Paris. Her skills proved valuable enough to secure a promotion to paid employee status, and in the years leading up to the German invasion of France, she was recognized as an asset to the museum.

Valland worked under Jacques Jaujard, Director of the Musees Nationeaux, when the Germans first invaded a large part of France, and along with collaborators in-country, established the Vichy government. The Nazis selected the Jan de Paume Museum to serve as an art repository and distribution site, and dubbed it the "Reich Leader Rosenberg Institute for the Occupied Territories".

(Hermann Goering selected artwork for his personal collection there.) Under the command of Otto Abetz, Germany's ambassador to Vichy France, the Nazis at the Institute photographed, inventoried, and distributed each piece with meticulous detail. Rose Valland was one of a very small group of museum staff, and eventually the only one, allowed to remain at her post as the Nazis carried out the operation. Under the guise of maintaining the building and collections, Janjard assigned Valland as "Special Staff for Pictorial Art".

Although she never studied German formally, Rose Valland understood the language perfectly well, but kept this fact secret from the Germans. She committed to memory information she gleaned while eavesdropping on the Germans during the day, and reputedly committed the information to paper after she returned home. Valland took negatives of the Nazi photos home at night, copied them, and returned them without detection. Virtually every record of intake and distribution was duplicated, and Valland transferred information to the French Resistance when possible. Indeed, she is sometimes referred to as the "mother of modern art" due to the integral role she played in alerting the Resistance and preventing a pending transport of modern art.

At the war's end, Valland was instrumental in advising the Monuments, Fine Arts and Archives Section (MFAA) of the Allied Forces, headed by American James Rorimer, of the fate of the Nazi plunder, including a substantial cache of priceless works uncovered from the Castle at Neuschwanstein. Among the valuables discovered there was the Gent altarpiece from the Van Eyck brothers, jewelry and furniture from the Rothschild family collection, and the gold and silver works of David-Weill. Valland served as a member of the "Commission for the Recovery of Works of Art" after the war, and later as Conservator of the Musees Nationeaux. She also chaired the "Commission for the Protection of Works of Art".

Valland was awarded French Legion of Honor, Commander of the Order of Arts and Letters, Medal de la Resistance, Officer's Cross of the Order of Merit of the Federal Republic of Germany (West Germany), and the U.S. Medal of Freedom.   Nevertheless, her contribution to cultural preservation is little known.   Had Rose Valland not made it her responsibility to catalogue the Nazi's thefts and relocation, the world would very well have lost some of the greatest creations of the human mind.

IV *Elsie Ott*
(1913-2006)

Elsie Ott was a pioneer of air medical evacuation. Though she was a complete novice on her first evacuation assignment, Elsie Ott helped prove that medical evaluation by air was not only possible, but likely would be more successful than ground transportation of the wounded. Her recommendations for preparing aircraft and personnel for such missions set the standard by which later flight nurses would be trained.

Elsie Ott was born in Smithtown, NY. In 1941, she joined the U.S. Army Air Force Nurse Corps, and was commissioned as a 2nd Lieutenant. She served in the United States briefly before being transferred to Karachi, India. In the early days of World War II, there was no such thing as an air ambulance. Nevertheless, the prevalence of airplanes made them ideal for troop movement, wounded or otherwise. As early as 1942, patient airlifts had been successfully completed in Alaska, Burma and New Guinea. However, there had been no organized effort to move wounded soldiers from the more active combat theaters where casualties tended to be higher. In Karachi, Ott was stationed with the First Troop Carrier Command (FTCC). The FTCC was charged with completing the first intercontinental air evacuation transport. The Army planned to utilize combat planes to transport wounded soldiers to better-equipped hospitals. For the inaugural mission, Elsie Ott, who had never before flown in an airplane, was chosen as the sole nurse to staff that flight. She earned her metaphorical wings on an arduous, nearly 11,000 mile trek across the globe.

Ott was given twenty-four hours' notice to equip a D-47 Air Transport Command plane for the evacuation mission.

Her available supplies were limited to the minor medical necessities found in an average first aid kit. Perhaps worse, despite an expected initial human cargo of five, the plane was equipped with only two cots anchored to the floor. Ott gathered comfort supplies for the trip as best she could – blankets, bandages, and whatever else was available on-hand with such short notice. Ott's evacuation plane, and many that came after hers, carried troops and supplies and thus could not display the Red Cross, signifying that its occupants were on a humanitarian mission. To an enemy, Ott's plane appeared no different than any aircraft equipped solely for warfare.

Ott's compatriot on the flight was a very capable medical technician, who unfortunately suffered from severe arthritis and thus rendered Ott the "muscle" for the flight as well. Patients were not evaluated by medical personnel prior to loading the aircraft. Thus, Ott and the medical technician evaluated and triaged injuries as patients arrived. The trip would take Ott from India to Saudi Arabia, Sudan, Ghana, the Ascension Islands, Belize, Puerto Rico, Florida, and Washington DC. Mid-route, the passengers were examined by physicians, and with additional patients on board, they were transferred to a better-equipped B-21 with eleven mattresses on board. Just as the necessary supplies were not sufficiently anticipated, many administrative roadblocks were unforeseen. Ott was forced to pay for food and other necessities out of her own pocket on stops that were held by Allied, but not necessarily U.S. forces. Eventually, she supported herself and sixteen or more patients.

When the flight reached Morrison Field in Florida, Ott found the base short on personnel. She helped move litters with wounded into the field hospital, then removed all the mattresses and linens and scoured the plane to disinfect it. After six and a half days, the flight arrived near Washington DC. It would have taken three months to make the same trip on land and by sea.

After completing her mission, Ott submitted a report to the Army suggesting several key preparations necessary for medical air evacuations. Ott recommended that flights be equipped with oxygen, sufficient bandaging and dressing, and extra coffee. For the modern mind, it is hard to comprehend that such items were overlooked. Notably, given the rigors of such missions, close quarters, and potentially unsanitary conditions, Ott advised that flight nurses be outfitted in pants rather than skirts.

For her service, Ott was recognized in 1943 with the first Air Medal given to a woman. In addition, the success of Ott's flight encouraged the Army to move forward in creating a flight evacuation school at Bowen Field, KY.

In addition to instructing nurses on medical protocols, the program's formal training included physical conditioning, crash procedures, survival training, and education on the impact of altitude. Ott, of course, had not had the benefit of such training. After her ground-breaking flight she requested and was admitted to the Bowen Field program and later in 1943 officially became part of the 803rd Military Air Evacuation Squad (MAES). The first flight nurse to graduate was actually 2nd Lieutenant Geraldine Dishroon, who in 1944 had the distinction of being on the first air evacuation team to land on Omaha Beach after D-Day.

Elsie Ott was promoted to Captain, and served in the Army until her discharge in 1946. In 1965, in honor of her legacy to the war effort Ott was selected to christen a new C-9 air ambulance the "Nightingale". Elsie Ott was indeed a key figure in the Army's success toward improving survival rates for soldiers wounded at the front. Of the nearly 1.2 million patients evacuated by air throughout the war, only 46 died en route.

V *Aleda Lutz*
(1915-1944)

Elsie Ott paved the way for Aleda Lutz to make her mark on history as perhaps the most successful of the two percent of nurses that served in World War II that were qualified as flight nurses. Lutz also has the unfortunate distinction of being the first American woman killed in action during World War II. As a result of her early death, there is a dearth of biographical information available for Aleda, if for no other reason than she did not have the privilege of recording her memoirs or writing her autobiography after the war concluded.   Nevertheless, by the time of Lutz's death, at the young age of twenty-eight, Lutz had flown more missions and helped save more lives than any of her contemporaries. Her story deserves to be told.

Lutz, from Freedland, MI, was the youngest of ten children, the only one to have graduated from high school. (Interestingly, and perhaps fittingly, the farm she grew up on later became part of the MBS International Airport.) Lutz enlisted in the Army Nurse Corps in 1942, commissioned as a 2nd Lieutenant and assigned as a general duty nurse at Selfridge Field in Clemens, MI. She was transferred for training to the 349th Air Evacuation Camp at Bowman Field then reassigned to the 802nd Medical Air Evacuation Transport Squadron and sent to North Africa. Lutz began flying combat missions in 1943 and was promoted to 1st Lieutenant.

She conducted all-weather medical evacuation flights in Tunisia, Italy, and France in 1943-1944. She is recorded as having flown four sorties in one day onto the beach head during the Battle of Anzio, which was part of the Winter Line and the Battle for Rome of the Allies' Italian Campaign. In the twenty months of her war career, Lutz earned six battle stars: Rome/Arno, Tunisia, Sicily, Naples Foggia, Southern France, and the North Apennines. Lutz transported over 3500 injured patients, ran 196 missions, and logged 814 combat hours, more than most combat pilots.

Her work on unmarked transport planes and at the front put her squarely in the line of fire, but it was weather that lead to her death in 1944. While travelling between Luxeuill and Istres as a member of the 51st Troop Carriers Wing, Lutz's Douglas Medevac C-47 encountered a violent storm. In the fog, rain, and frost, the pilots lost his bearings. The two-engine aircraft crashed near St. Chaumon, France on the side of Mont Pleasant, the highest mountain in the westernmost part of the Mercantour national park. She was the only woman on board, and perished with the four crew members, nine U.S. Soldiers, and six German POWs. A monument to Lutz is erected near the crash site. Lutz is the only woman buried in the Rhone American Cemetery in Draguignan, France.

Lutz was awarded four Air Medals (medal and three Oak Leaf Clusters), a Red Cross medal, and the Purple Heart. She was posthumously given the Distinguished Flying Cross, the second given to a woman after Amelia Earhart, "for outstanding proficiency and selfless devotion to duty". Soon after her death, the Army christened an 800-patient hospital ship the USAHS *Aleda E. Lutz*. The ship was dedicated by Secretary of the Army General George C. Marshall. A medical evacuation aircraft was also christened after Lutz as "Miss Nightingale III".

In 1949, a member of the U.S. Congress proposed to rename the Veteran's Affairs facility in Saginaw, MI after Aleda Lutz. The initiative did not succeed. This is likely because she was a female veteran among a sea of hundreds of thousands of men that had also served their country. Nevertheless, almost fifty years later President George H.W. Bush renamed the VA facility in her honor. It was the first time such an installation was christened in honor of a woman. Lutz's uniform and medals are displayed at the hospital.

Aleda Lutz's life was brief but meaningful. Not only did she show that women were up to the task of successfully serving in war zones, she helped ensure that thousands of families saw their fighting men and boys return. She gave her life to make that happen.

VI Susan Travers
(1909-2003)

Susan Travers was a very real person, but one can imagine her in an adventure film as the supporting character who utterly steals the show. The only woman ever to officially join the French Foreign Legion, Travers not only showed courage under fire, she may in fact have had a pivotal role in turning the war in North Africa in the favor of the Allies.

Born in London in 1909, Travers was thought of as an "adventurer" even as a girl. Adventure was likely in her blood. Her father was Royal Navy Admiral Francis Eaton Travers, and her paternal grandfather was a statesman who served as British Consul in Marseilles. In fact, during World War I, Travers' father was put in charge of marine transport at Marseilles, where his own father had been stationed, and in 1921 the family moved to Cannes. There, Travers lived a life of relative luxury. She is sometimes described as having been a playgirl, but this may be a typically disrespectful assessment of a well-to-do young woman of the times. In fact, she was talented enough, and dedicated enough to compete on the tennis circuit at the semi-professional level, and even competed at the Wimbledon Tennis tournament.

At the outset of World War II, Susan Travers passed the necessary tests to secure a nursing diploma so that she might become an ambulance driver – a job for which such training was required. After she'd secured her position as a driver, Travers Joined the French Expeditionary Force to Finland's Winter War with the Soviet Union in 1939-1940. During her time in Scandinavia, France fell to the Nazis.

Travers made her way back to England and joined De Gaulle's Free French Forces. Travers wanted nothing further to do with nursing, considering it "too messy", and embraced a persona as a fearless ambulance driver. She served as a chauffeur in the 13th Demi Brigade of the French Foreign Legion in Syria, and later was sent to North Africa to drive senior military officials.

Travers became chauffeur to Colonel Marie-Pierre Koenig , who had been sent to defend Bir Hakeim in Libya to prevent the Germans from reaching Cairo and thus controlling access to the Suez Canal. Field Marshall Erwin Rommel's German and Italian Afrika Korps had laid siege to North Africa for months, and the Allies were in threat of a defeat. Travers and her colleagues witnessed the abortive attack on Dakar, in French West Africa (now Senegal) and expected a severe battle for Bir Hakeim. Females were ordered out of the area, and Travers was temporarily forced to leave.

While waiting for Rommel's inevitable advance, but seeing no evidence of an immediate assault, Koenig (with whom Travers was also romantically involved) let Travers return to Bir Hakeim. She was there and the only woman on duty when Rommel attacked in 1942.

Overly confident and severely underestimating the mettle of the entrenched Allies and Legionnaires, Field Marshall Rommel had told his troops the siege would take fifteen minutes. Colonel Marie-Pierre Koenig and the Legionnaires instead held out for fifteen days against Rommel's artillery and tanks, until their ammunition, food, and water were exhausted. They were forced to retreat. It was at this juncture that Travers played a key part in the Foreign Legion troops' escape from Rommel.

Despite being effectively surrounded, Koenig determined to lead a breakout at night through three concentric cordons of German panzers. It was Susan Travers, in fact, that drove the car that lead 2400 Allied troops, including 650 Legionnaires, in retreat through German minefields and machine-gun fire. Driving blindly in the dark, Travers drove through multiple German brigades, and literally ran into a group of parked panzers. Nevertheless, she made it to Allied ground, and in the course of the escape set the tone for the Allies' resolve, against all odds, to prevail.

After her service in North Africa, Travers served in Italy (with the U.S. 5th Army), France, and Germany, driving ambulances, trucks, and even a self-propelled anti-tank gun. During a return visit to Bir Hakeim later in the war, Travers was wounded by a mine that exploded beneath her vehicle, but recovered.

Nicknamed "La Miss" by the troops, Travers' fearlessness at Bir Hakeim was recognized throughout Free France, and she was subsequently awarded the Legion d'Honneur, Croix de Guerre, Medaille Militaire and the Ordre du Corps, d'Arme. Koenig himself was lavished with praise and went on to become a hero of France, known as the man that helped change the face of Rommel's North Africa campaign.

After World War II, Travers enrolled in the *Legion Etrangere* as an Adjutant Chef. She is the only woman to join the French Foreign Legion officially, having omitted her gender from the application. Travers was an officer in the logistics division, and she designed and adopted her own uniform since women's gear was not produced. She served in Vietnam during the First Indochine War. Travers married Adjutant-Chef Nicholas Schlegelmulck who also fought in 13th Demi Brigade in North Africa. In 1956, when she was awarded the Medaille Militaire, it was Marie-Pierre Koenig, then Minister of Defence, who pinned her lapel.

Travers kept detailed diaries of her experiences during World War II, but shortly after war's end she destroyed them. Working from memory, after her husband, Koenig, and other principals died, Travers published *Tomorrow to Be Brave: A Memoire of the Only Woman Ever to Serve in the French Foreign Legion*, which recounted her exploits as the "daredevil ambulance driver", and revealed details of the personal relationships she developed during the war with Koenig and others. Travers also shared credit for driving through the Bir Hakeim assault with Koenig, whom she said at some point had taken the wheel. Even so, Travers' heroism on that drive in Bir Hakeim is no less significant or important. The significance does not come from her time behind the wheel, nor because she was a woman. She possessed a level of bravery that few mortals can muster.

VII   *Eileen Nearne* (1921-2010)

Jacqueline Nearne (1916-1982)

The "Fighting Sullivans" are well-known American heroes of World War II, and the family is recognized as having made the ultimate sacrifice in a single battle when all five brothers aboard the light carrier U.S.S. Juneau were killed. Thousands of families made similar commitments and are less well-known, despite the fact that their contributions to the war effort too helped secure, if not ensure, victory for the Allies. The Nearne family is one of those families. What makes the family unique is that two of its familial fighters were sisters Eileen and Jacqueline, who risked their lives to save France along with their brother Francis. Both assigned by the Special Operations Executive (SOE) to France, the sisters played a key role in freeing their adopted country from Nazi control.

The Nearnes were born in England to an English father and French-Spanish mother (they had another brother who did not serve in the war). The family moved to France in 1923, and all children were raised speaking French fluently.

At the onset of World War II, older sister Jacqueline had experience working as a travelling office equipment representative, but neither she nor any of the siblings had done anything of notable consequence. When their English heritage became too suspicious to the Germans in France, and perhaps became more meaningful to the Nearnes given the geopolitical circumstances, the family made its way back to England.

Jacqueline Nearne initially applied to be a driver with the women's Auxiliary Territorial Service, but was rejected for lack of experience as a driver, and particularly because she was not accustomed to driving on the left side of the road. As fluent French speakers, Jacqueline and Eileen's potential value to British intelligence operations in France was quickly recognized, and the two sisters were recruited by the SOE. The women underwent parachute training and were further trained in Morse code, wireless transmission, evasion tactics, and weaponry. They were also instructed on silent killing techniques, including using a special double edged dagger called a Fairbairn Sykes.

While Jacqueline's intelligence and skill were recognized early, Eileen was not initially as well-received by SOE superiors, who questioned her capacity and readiness for the mission. Nevertheless, of 3200 women who took up arms in service to SOE, Jacqueline and Eileen were two of forty dropped into Occupied France. Eileen worked as a wireless operator; Jacqueline worked as a courier. Both successful at their missions, their fates proved to be radically dissimilar.

Eileen worked other jobs initially, including as a home-based signals operator, but in 1944 parachuted into occupied territory to work as a wireless operator for the Wizard network of Operation Mitchel (and later worked for the Spiritualist network). Her cover was as a member of the First Aid Nursing Yeomanry. In this role, she helped local Resistance leader, Jean Savy, set up the network, and was tasked with finding and organizing financial support and resources for the French Resistance. To say the least, it was a dangerous job. The Germans employed radio-detecting vans to trace the signals of the Allies' spies; thus, the average SOE wireless operator lasted just six weeks before being arrested.

Eileen is noted for having evaded detection and/or arrest for five months – over twice the average successful in-service rate for wireless operators. During that time, she transmitted 105 messages to British intelligence with information related to German troop and weapons movements. She proved to be a convincing liar and several times talked her way out of arrest, the first time convincing her Gestapo detainer that she was merely an innocent "shop girl". Her luck eventually ran out as her transmitter was detected and she was arrested in 1944.

Nevertheless, before her capture, she managed to destroy all evidence of the messages sent and hid her wireless device. The Germans found no physical evidence of Eileen the spy, and she maintained her innocence, claiming that she was unwittingly duped into sending messages for a British businessman whom she said was the spy.

Eileen's captors, of course, refused to believe her story. She was taken in and mercilessly tortured by the German state police (Gestapo), including by "treatment of the bath", which is similar to the modern tactic of "waterboarding". She was sent to Ravensbruck concentration camp, but refused to do prison work, and was subsequently transferred to several labor camps during her captivity. However, on a forced march near Markkleeberg, Eileen escaped from her work detail. She was arrested by the SS but as she had done throughout her internment, Eileen claimed innocence and she was released. Hidden by a priest until liberation, Eileen never revealed her true identity, SOE role, or any other intelligence that put SOE operations or the Allies at risk. She was mistaken for a Nazi spy by Allied liberators, but once her story was identified, she was released and transported back to England.

Though similarly at risk of discovery and execution, Jacqueline Nearne served in Occupied France for an astounding fifteen months before being safely recalled to London. She was the first woman (with Odette Sansom) to train at Training School 51 Ringway Parachute School. In 1943, she parachuted into France to work for the "Stationer" Circuit, and also maintained contact with the nearby "Headmaster" network. Jacqueline's cover was also that of a member of the First Aid Nursing Yeomanry, but in truth she was a courier for Stationer leader Maurice Southgate. Jacqueline clandestinely passed messages, was directly involved with sabotage of German infrastructure (blowing up pylons, railway lines, factories) and communications, transferring troop intelligence to the Allies, and relaying weapons information. She purportedly carried spare radio parts in her cosmetics bag despite the incredible risk to her life had her possession of such equipment been discovered. Maurice Buckmaster, the leader of the French section of SOE, referred to Jacqueline as on one of the best agents in France.

After the war, Eileen and Jacqueline's lives converged, but once again their post-war experiences, just like their war-time records, proved to be vastly different. Eileen was awarded the Croix de Guerre, and also made a Member of the Order of the British Empire (MBE). Jacqueline, who was also awarded the MBE, actually starred in an SOE –produced documentary film *Now It Can Be Told*, which indeed told the story of agents' war-time exploits. Jacqueline went on to work for the United Nations. Her portrait, by fellow SOE operative, Brian Stonehouse, hangs in the Special Forces Club in London.

Eileen, by contrast, kept her SOE past secret. It is very likely Eileen suffered from a mental illness before the war, but her capture and torture most certainly brought about psychological distress.

She was frequently cared for by older sister Jacqueline, and spent some time in a mental treatment facility where she underwent electroshock therapy in pursuit of relief.

She is known to have spoken only once publicly about her war-time service, in a French documentary where she was interviewed in disguise. She died reclusive and relatively unknown in 2010. However, once her identity and history became known, Eileen's family and historians made great efforts to ensure her incredible bravery and unassailable patriotism would not continue unacknowledged.

VIII *Claire Phillips*
(1908-1960)

Claire Phillips is sometimes referred to as the "American Mata Hari". Under the guise of a good-time club owner and entertainer, Phillips collected information from Japanese service members and transmitted the intelligence to Allied forces in the Pacific.

Phillips was born Claire Snyder in 1907 in Michigan She is one of few youngsters that actually did run away from home to join the circus, taking a job selling tickets to a snake charmer's show. Claire had theater and showmanship in her blood, and in her twenties moved to Manila and toured with a musical company throughout the Philippines, which was America's largest colony. There she met and married sailor Manuel Fuentes and had a daughter. The trio moved briefly to Portland OR, but the marriage was short-lived. After Claire and Manuel divorced, Claire took her daughter and returned to the Philippines to join a dance troupe. In 1941 she married John Phillips, an American Soldier. The Japanese had attacked Pearl Harbor, and Clair's husband retreated with the Army to the hills outside Manila. Claire followed, and lived in the hills close to him, surviving as did the others on wild game, snakes, and monkeys. After the Japanese invaded, John Phillips was captured. He later died in a Japanese prison camp.

The Americans surrendered in 1942. Phillips was then recruited into espionage by an American, John Boone, who coincidentally had been a theater agent before the war. Phillips intended to support the Philippine resistance, but the spy ring she formed also passed information to the Americans in the Pacific theater.

Philips worked with Fely Corcuera, a fellow dancer, to invent a persona as Philippine-born Italian dancer "Dorothy Clara Fuentes". Together, she and Corcuera established the Tsubaki cabaret club in Manila. The club was patronized by Japanese officers who came to see the dance reviews as maturely staged for a gentleman's club. Claire Phillips proved to be the consummate hostess, and it became commonplace for the officers to share privileged information to the dancing spy. Each night Phillips would write up intelligence gleaned from the evening's patrons and messenger the information to General Douglas MacArthur and his cadre of leaders in the Pacific. Claire later claimed that information she shared lead to the annihilation of an entire Japanese sub squadron.

In addition to her spying, Phillips functioned as a smuggler to the Cabanatuan prison. She smuggled food, medical supplies, and information to POWs, and garnered the nickname "High Pockets" after revealing that she frequently transported messages in her brassiere. In 1944 one of her messengers was captured carrying a message from Phillips to the Allies and killed. Phillips' cover was blown, and she was arrested by Kempeitai, the Japanese equivalent of the Gestapo.

Phillips was taken to Bilibid POW camp and prison in Manila and tortured by her Japanese captors. She refused to give up any information and endured solitary confinement for six months. Phillips was slated to be executed, but had her death sentence commuted to twelve years of hard labor.

Phillips was liberated by American troops in 1945, near death from starvation. After her recovery, she published a memoir of her war-time exploits, *Manila Espionage*.

Her story was adapted as a Hollywood movie, *I Was an American Spy*, starring Ann Dvorak.

Phillips advised on the production of the biographical film, undoubtedly relishing her connection to Hollywood. She was a guest on This Is Your Life on March 15, 1950. In Portland, she was lavished with praise, and local community leaders ensured she was given a house, a free car, and promised paid tuition for her daughter at the local college. In 1951, Claire Phillips was awarded the Medal of Freedom on the recommendation of General MacArthur himself.

Her post-war life did not prove as successful as it might have, however. Claire Phillips later sued the U.S. government unsuccessfully for $146,850 in compensation for her services and for reimbursement of the expenses she incurred in the Pacific. The U.S. Claims Court accused Phillips of fabricating her story; she was awarded only $1349. She died suddenly of meningitis in 1960, nearly destitute.

IX *Nancy Wake*

(1912-2011)

Nancy Wake was a spy, a guerilla leader and fighter, and a trained killer. She was a fearless leader of Maquis Resistance groups in Occupied France, and recruited a force of 7,500 volunteers to fight against the Germans.

Born in New Zealand in 1912, Nancy Wake was the youngest of six children in an impoverished family that her father abandoned soon after her birth. Relocated to Sydney as a youth, Nancy ran away to become a nurse at sixteen. Later, Wake made her way to London and trained as journalist, subsequently working in Vienna and Paris as a European correspondent. In 1937, Wake married French industrialist Henri Fiocca and thereafter undertook a life of high society that contrasted sharply with her origins. They lived in Marseille at the time of the German invasion.

Nancy Wake became a courier for the Resistance and joined the escape network of Captain Ian Ganon as an escort. Between 1940 and 1943, she was credited with saving the lives of hundreds of Allied soldiers and airmen by escorting them from occupied France to Spain.

She was forced to flee Marseilles when the network was exposed in 1943, and her husband who'd remained behind was captured and executed by the Gestapo. Nancy herself was arrested briefly but managed to escape to Spain. Upon reaching London, Wake joined the SOE.

After training, Nancy parachuted into Auvergne, where she served as a liaison between SOE headquarters and Henri Tardivat in the Forest of Troncais.

Her duties in Auvergne included allocating weapons, equipment and finances. However, she was more combatant than administrator: Nancy Wake led attacks on Gestapo headquarters in Montlucon, and reportedly killed an SS sentry with her bare hands to keep him quiet. Once she made a three hundred mile bike ride through German-held territories to replace lost wireless codes, passing through multiple enemy checkpoints along the way. Fittingly, though they could not otherwise identify her, the Gestapo called her "White Mouse" in recognition of her ability to escape. Nancy Wake was the Gestapo's most-wanted person with a 5 million franc reward on her head. Miraculously, she operated without detection until the end of the war.

For her service, Nancy Wake was awarded the George Medal, Medal of Freedom, Medeille de la Resistance, 3x Croix de Guerre, Companion of the Order of Australia, RSA Badge in Gold from New Zealand, and the Legion of Honor. She worked for the British Air Ministry in international embassies in Paris and Prague. Later, she moved to Sydney, where she ran unsuccessfully for several government positions. Wake married RAF Officer John Forward, and lived alternately in England and Australia for many years. Her autobiography, *The White Mouse*, was published in 1985.

X *Vera Atkins*

(1908-2000)

Vera Atkins lived to lead a secret life. A noted Anglophile, Atkins, who served in the SOE from 1941-1945, was actually a naturalized British citizen born a Romanian Jew. She kept her origins secret from her colleagues in the intelligence world, and harbored much graver secrets that could've put her career in jeopardy, and did in fact cause rumors of treasonous activity. Regardless, Vera Atkins is recognized as a heroine for her successful handling of scores of SOE agents in France during World War II, as well as for her post-war tenacity in documenting the fates of missing and lost agents.

Vera Atkins was born Vera-May Rosenberg in Crasna, Romania, which is now part of Ukraine. The Rosenbergs were a well-to-do family in the timber business, and Vera lived a relative life of privilege. It is known that she was a friend of anti-Nazi German ambassador Friedrich Werner von der Schulenberg, and it's suspected that she at least had access to many diplomats in Romania who were surreptitious British agents.

Atkins studied at the Sorbonne briefly and trained at Secretarial School in London before officially emigrating to Britain in 1937. At the outset of the war, Atkins volunteered as an Air Raid Precautions Warden in Chelsea. In 1941, Vera joined the French section of SOE as a secretary. Later she became assistant to F-Section leader, Colonel Maurice Buckmaster. By virtue of this position, Atkins acted as an intelligence officer, though unofficially until after her British citizenship was secured in 1944.

Atkins was noted to have an exceptional memory, and Buckmaster clearly respected Atkins' abilities. Buckmaster gave Atkins supervisory authority over all thirty-seven female agents in France. As the agents' handler, Atkins administered support for them, processed cover for the agents' assumed identities, and famously waved them off at the airfield as they departed for France.

The Germans tried and were almost successful at destroying the SOE's networks in France while Atkins and her boss Buckminster did their best to keep the operation whole. Despite the fact that there was a series of identity checks and protocols required to be followed in order to communicate with an F-Section agent in the field, the Germans were notoriously successful at using captured SOE agents' radios to infiltrate the networks, and Buckmaster, along with Vera Atkins, had been accused of being lax in verifying agents' identities. The Germans took down SOE networks in the Netherlands and Belgium; however, Buckmaster and Atkins were not informed of this collapse.

Buckmaster is believed to have ignored a message that had no check and later failed to give credence to a message that indicated that multiple agents had been captured by the Germans. Thus, he and Atkins unwittingly gave the Germans valuable intelligence that risked the lives, and ended some, of the F-Section agents on the ground.

Following her naturalization, Atkins was in 1944 commissioned as a Flight Officer in the Women's Auxiliary Air Force (WAAF), then officially appointed an F-Section intelligence officer. In January 1946 Atkins was brought on by the Secret Intelligence Service (MI6) and was promoted to the Squadron Office in the Women's Auxiliary Air Force. Concerned for the fate of her agents, Atkins made it her mission to uncover the details of the 118 agents missing in France.

She travelled to France and Germany, visited labor camps, and concentration camps, and even interrogated Nazi leaders such as Auschwitz-Birkenau Commandant Rudolph Hoess (then in custody) to glean information about the agents. In all, Atkins traced the fate of 117 of 118 missing agents and detailed the deaths of fourteen women agents, twelve of whom were murdered in concentration camps. Atkins pursuaded the War Office to identify those twelve agents as "killed in action", and over many years worked to have plaques set for each of the twelve women murdered. For her service, and her success in documenting the circumstances of many agents' deaths, Atkins was nominated for but was not awarded an MBE following the war. In 1948, she was awarded the Croix de Guerre. Year later, she received the Legion d'Honneur (1995) and was made a CBE (1997).

Post-war, Atkins worked for UNESCO's Central Bureau for Educational Visits and Exchanges ultimately becoming director. She retired in 1961. Atkins also served as an advisor on several films and biographies of SOE F-Section agents. Though she wished to have the SOE stories told accurately, she kept her own obscured, even persuading MRD Foot not to include the details of her Jewish-Romanian origins in his official SOE history.

Atkins' murky past, and her role in the near-failure of F-Section's intelligence networks in France lead some to question whether Atkins herself was a double agent, either working for the Germans or the Soviet Union. Interestingly, it was known that Atkins had been in the German-occupied Netherlands before she arrived in Britain, ostensibly trapped there trying to secure the escape of a cousin. Atkins biographer Sarah Helm (*A Life in Secrets*) revealed the truth of her actions in 2006 after discovering evidence indicating that Atkins paid a Nazi double-agent to help her cousin escape. The cousin was then obligated to spy for the Germans.

Perhaps it is the knowledge that in saving her family member Atkins indirectly supported Germany that caused her to work so tirelessly after the war to bring closure to the families of missing agents. Regardless, her heroism and dedication to the SOE colleagues that she sent into the field cannot be denied. Incidentally, Vera Atkins was a cousin of Rudolph Vrba, who escaped from Auschwitz early in the war, and provided the Allies with the first evidence of the conditions in Nazi concentration camps. Clearly Vera and her kin deserve much credit for shedding light on the consequence of the war.

References and Further Reading

Adamson, Lynda G. *Notable Women in American History: A Guide to Recommended Biographies and Autobiographies*. Westport, CT: Greenwood, 1999.

Albert-Lake, Virginia D' *An American Heroine in the French Resistance: The Diary and Memoir of Virginia D'Albert-Lake*. Ed. Judy Barrett Litoff. New York: Fordham UP, 2006. World War II--the Global, Human, and Ethical Dimension.

Bimberg, Edward L. *Tricolor over the Sahara: The Desert Battles of the Free French, 1940-1942*. Westport, CT: Greenwood, 2002.

Bouchoux, Corrinne. *Rose Valland: Resistance At the Museum*. Laurel Publishing, LLC, 2013.

Bourke-White, Margaret. *Portrait of Myself*. New York: Simon & Schuster, 1963.

Breuer, William B. *War and American Women: Heroism, Deeds, and Controversy*. Westport, CT: Praeger, 1997.

Brooks, Tim. *British Propaganda to France, 1940-1944: Machinery, Method and Message*. Edinburgh: Edinburgh UP, 2007. International Communications.

Goldman, Nancy Loring, ed. *Female Soldiers--Combatants or Noncombatants?: Historical and Contemporary Perspectives*. Westport, CT: Greenwood, 1982.

Holsinger, M. Paul, and Mary Anne Schofield, eds. *Visions of War: World War II in Popular Literature and Culture*. Bowling Green, OH: Bowling Green State U Popular, 1992.

Howe, Thomas Carr, Jr. *Salt Mines and Castles: The Discovery and Restitution of Looted European Art*. Indianapolis: Bobbs-Merrill, 1946.

Jackson, Kathi. *They Called Them Angels: American Military Nurses of World War II*. Westport, CT: Praeger, 2000.

Karlsgodt, Elizabeth Campbell. *Defending National Treasures: French Art and Heritage under Vichy*. Stanford, CA: Stanford UP, 2011.

Levine, Alan J. *Captivity, Flight, and Survival in World War II*. Westport, CT: Praeger, 2000. .

Phillips, Claire and Myron B. Goldsmith. *Manila Espionage*. Binford and Mort, 1947.

Rasor, Eugene L. *The Southwest Pacific Campaign, 1941-1945: Historiography and Annotated Bibliography*. Westport, CT: Greenwood, 1996.

Street, Nancy Lynch, and Marilyn J. Matelski, eds. *Messages from the Underground: Transnational Radio in Resistance and in Solidarity*. Westport, CT: Praeger, 1997.

Travers, Susan and Wendy Holden. *Tomorrow to Be Brave: A Memoir of the Only Woman Ever to Serve in the French Foreign Legion*. Touchstone, 2007.

Vomécourt, Philippe De. *An Army of Amateurs*. Garden City, NY: Doubleday, 1961.

Wake, Nancy. The White Mouse. Macmillan, 1986.

Conclusion

Thank you for purchasing this book, I hope you enjoyed learning about these fantastically brave women and have a greater understanding of just how invaluable these women were to the success of the war.

If you have enjoyed the book, I would be most grateful if you could spare sometime to please leave a review.

Thank you.

CPSIA information can be obtained
at www.ICGtesting.com
Printed in the USA
LVHW082232240820
664077LV00037B/3101